Some Wild Woman

poems by

Esther Sadoff

Finishing Line Press
Georgetown, Kentucky

Some Wild Woman

For my mother

ACKNOWLEDGMENTS

Atticus Review: My mother slips scarves into my hand
Bluestem: My mother on vacation
Cagibi: My mother when company comes
Cathexis Northwest Press: My mother cracks watermelons into halves
Death Rattle / Oroboro Lit Journal: My mother at the exhibition
Hawaii Pacific Review: My mother jerks the wheel left then right
Hole in the Head Review: My mother always says yes; I never saw my mother
on a hike; My mother tells me to enjoy; My mother doesn't understand tears;
My mother scolds me for what?
Little Patuxent Review: My mother watches birds at the cracked fountain
Midway Journal: My mother spins the compost
Pidgeonholes: My mother chucks muck from the gutter
Red Ogre Review: On the beach, my mother and father walked hand in hand
Sierra Nevada Review: My mother always has something for me
Up the Staircase Quarterly: I don't know if my mother always loved horses

Publisher: Leah Huete de Maines
Editor: Christen Kincaid
Cover Art and Design: Original oil painting by Esther Sadoff
Author Photo: Esther Sadoff

Order online: www.finishinglinepress.com
also available on amazon.com

Author inquiries and mail orders:
Finishing Line Press
PO Box 1626
Georgetown, Kentucky 40324
USA

Contents

My mother chucks muck from the gutter

leans one foot swinging over nothing,
ignores storm clouds, the ladder
gone rickety over rocks until the drain
sputters and shocks, a gush of brown
water gone clear. She pours coffee water
over spider plants, and once nearly chucked
the bucket at a high-hanging aloe before I stopped her.
She wipes down spider webs and dust
without looking, rinses clumps in the white sink.
I imagine her walking away from my father,
declaring him a baby, she three years his senior.
She drifted down the gray beach away from him.
How she said *Not in your mother's house* and
Not unless you are a doctor. How she'd wait
another three years, teach him to get things done.

My mother watches birds at the cracked fountain

When a feral cat keeps gifting my sister shredded robin wings,
she says *Oh well*, declares the robins *so mean*.
She's befuddled by dogs, but could excuse any cat,
so like herself the years she divested herself
of friends and went dancing in New York City clubs alone,
a smooth-talker waiting for her when she returned to her chair.
How she leaned at the piano, never brought any boys home,
kept all the gifts: a necklace with a shiny letter *K*,
the glowing stud earrings.
She bangs on the window to startle the squirrels,
the presumptuous robin gobbling seeds,
like she bangs on the piano,
sound blasting so loudly I can't hear a thing.

After two days on vacation, my mother calls me troubled

Not sure what she is doing there.
By the time she comes back,
the door is open for the constant flux
of piano students trampling in and out.
In between, she bags weeds and sticks,
goes in and out amidst the television's dull roar.
She snatches whatever I've thrown
in the trash and puts it in the compost:
potato parings and delicate shells crushed under the lid.
At dinner, she carves away the meat and keeps
the bone under the guise she likes it best,
squeezes slices of lemon on the counters,
down the drain, steals my glass of water to give to the plants.
She has two of everything and gives me both,
like the time she clutched a set of porcelain butter knives—
a flurry of protestations while I slammed the door,
only to find them in my bag, placed when no one was looking.

My mother cracks watermelon into halves

scoops out the center until its flesh pales to white.
Later sips the cool liquid from the rind.
She eats cherries by the handful,
cups orange and clementine skins
in the shadow of the TV, splits pistachios
and scatters shells across the table.
She's always in the yard, unclogging some obstruction.
I show her videos of flooded backyards being drained,
the water sputtering and descending with a jolt.
She fears those raucous waters, the rocking of a boat.
Panics as my father pulls in and out of the dock.
She rushes home over the slippery path,
watches for fear the boat has gone crooked again.
She cracks open a watermelon for me
as if I only came for its sweetness, the gem of its red heart.

My mother always says yes

Gives her house keys away for the weekend,
makes up the bed for anyone in town,
rolls out trays of cheese and crackers,
gives pizza to the piano students before the lesson.
For years, the driveway was darkened by other people's cars,
the television by small, unwelcome heads.
We parked in the street and fumed up the stairs.
So at 35, I practice saying *No* when my sister asks me to trek
across the country with two giant Halloween spiders.
My mother lends me a suitcase, the spiders already inside.
Laid flat they take up no room she says.
I wonder if I could take up less room.
At my sister's house, the spiders creep up
the still-warm bricks. At my sister's house,
all my *Nos* eye me in the dark.

I never saw my mother on a hike

My father dreams about the coast,
dreams about the shoreline
with its crisp, dry air. Takes photos
of lakes and ocean. Never river or stream.
He never liked to hike or camp,
so I never saw my mother
in a shower of golden leaves,
my mother shaking down a stick
or walking by a stream until now.
My mother manages the trees,
the jagged, unruly branches.
Tries to quicken a mucky flow with her foot.
When a tree branch falls into
the muddy trail she tries to lift it.
She always loved a clear path,
a straight way forward.

My mother tells me to enjoy

On Fridays, she and my father go out to eat.
She orders one of everything for half-price.
It's time to try bowls of mussels
cracked open mid-sigh, snaked ridges of sushi,
crusted rings and squiggles of calamari.
She watches me as I take a bite,
tells me *Things can still be good*
though I notice only the edges of things,
the saltiness, the sweetness,
never the substance. I gaze at
the blankness of the open balcony,
I wonder how to enjoy with such gusto,
how to find anything succulent.
I eat smile nod. I try to cheer up.
She makes me *show up show up show up.*

My mother doesn't understand tears

I've never seen her cry or be sick,
just once her face gone gray behind the door.
My mother doesn't know weakness.
At the end of a piano recital,
she slaps each child on the back,
declares *We've got work to do.*
Now when she slaps me on the back
I think *I need to toughen up.*
Maybe all those times I said *No*
with the fierce blankness of tears,
she never saw me cry, saw only
the work, the open sheets of music.
Each time I think I've made my last
refusal, I sit on the bench and play.

My mother scolds me for what?

When she gets a mischievous gleam in her eye
and looks like she's about to tell me a secret,
I know what she's about to say.
My sigh is hers. My laugh is hers.
The way I swear under my breath is hers.
I speak with my grandmother's voice,
a speech I know I must have forgotten,
and yet in the imprint of my brain
is my grandmother muttering *Goodnight*
as a curse plus a hail of unchoice words.
Even the way I hunch with worry,
shake my head in grief, or clench the steering,
chest pressed practically to the wheel
is *hers hers hers*. My mother's just here to say it.

My mother wakes up fuming

Messages my sister about love.
You can't teach a man to come.
You can't teach a man to sit still.
My mother has a jealous eye.
Watches my father swim laps in the pool,
glances at the curvy woman
with goggles paddling nearby.
She loves to hear my father talk,
but scolds his impracticality.
Lately, she says *yes* more and more.
How many things can a man be denied?
But to my mother, you can only say yes,
though sometimes I try to say nothing.
My father says she has the bite of a junkyard dog.
Once she holds on, she never lets go.

My mother is always cleaning

She lifts dust from the tables,
scoops up egg shells and chopped onions,
lets the dishes soak in the sink,
a film of omelet like a sunrise on each plate.
She shows me the drawers she's emptied,
tasks me with emptying one more.
I quickly dispose of old bookmarks,
buttons, tags, twenty-year-old
receipts my sister wants us to save.
Now when I come over, I no longer point
at the orange juice left out since morning,
a stick of butter melting in the sun.
My father prefers it this way.
As if keeping the piles of pots and pans,
stacks of papers on the floor,
drawers brimming with old toys,
were a way to preserve my mother.

My mother slips scarves into my hand

Shows me hats, gloves, asks me
to keep them or put them in the bag
with the discarded, sullen few.
Every day we try to fill a bag.
We sneak in my sister's old scarves
though she's miles away,
won't even notice they're gone.
I don't envy the tattered fabrics,
the dust-worn wool, the frayed and waving tassels,
each item a year I don't mind forgetting.
Next we switch to my mother's closet:
layers of black clothing so dark
we can't find a thing. When I refuse
to take anything home, she meets me outside
with cakes and a hat I've never seen before.
When my parents visit my sister, they call me,
place the phone where I should be sitting,
and declare *We're all together again.*

On the beach, my mother and father walked hand in hand

My grandmother leaned against the railing,
a tempestuous cloud over her face.
In quiet tones, she painted my mother a wild woman,
as if she were saying something we didn't know:
my mother spraying cold water on my sister
until she lifted the violin to her shoulder.
How she kicked me off the piano bench,
until I found my way to reason.
I marched my fingers up and down
silent desks and tables to pass the time,
fingers turned soldiers, fingers turned petal-soft.
In the quietest room I played scales
when no one was looking, closed the piano lid
so no one would hear, hid my flaws until the floor
trembled, my mother sliding in beside me,
clearing her throat. How the wash of water
resembles a rush of black and white keys.
I wanted to storm, be some wild woman.

My mother's jerks the wheel left then right

stops in the middle of the roundabout
under the pretense she wants to make
sure oncoming traffic has stopped
and I'm not sure anymore whether she understands
the purpose of the roundabout
or whether she's stopping for spite,
to prove to us she really *is* the queen of the road.
When she takes a turn, she yanks the wheel
one-handed and it takes everything
I have to hold onto my seat.
Down the road we sputter, drag, accelerate,
the car full of rattling cups, nectarine pits,
an apple that has been rolling in the trunk for days.
She lauds the car's safety features,
tells my father it's the *only* car she can drive.
My father tells my sister to find a man
with his own safety features.
Bells and whistles to beep and light up
if he starts to drift out of his lane.
We keep our eyes on the road when my mother drives,
though she's never had an accident in her life
and no one else in the car can say the same.

I don't know if my grandfather earned a college degree

but I do know he studied accounting.
He always asked my grandmother
to announce the grade he earned to everyone
and whether it *actually was* a B+ or an A- doesn't matter.
He always wore a suit and sang strange songs
that I only remember for their foreignness
and he may have sung them in a different language
for as much as my memory fails me.
I do know he sang *Big Girls Don't Cry*
to dry the impossible wave of my tears.
I do know he bought real-estate and hotels
and he was the *super*. Sometimes my mother knocked
on doors throughout the city to help collect the rent.
I imagine him strolling city streets in a gray suit,
hair greased back with slick and tufted curls,
declaring each familiar face a friend.
I know he probably yearned for straight hair.
I know he declared himself the son of the Queen of England
though he came from a place she would *never* have ventured.
I know he gambled, lost, and occasionally won.
That he refused to listen to my grandmother,
sold it all on a whim. I know he earned an A+ in accounting
or at least that's what my grandmother always said.

My mother has a second sight for happiness

Maybe that's why I rush under her gaze,
busy my hands and my feet,
though I tell her there's no such thing.
Sometimes I imagine happiness is like a parachute.
Some days my parachute is full
and I call her talking a mile a minute.
Together we rush to stores, fill the shopping cart
with jars and cans, drooping bags of spinach,
perspiring jugs of milk, dried fruit and nuts for my father.
I rush the cart back and help carry the bags
into the house where I lug them onto the counter.
She makes phone call after phone call,
asking *What's your news?* but we all talk so often
that no one ever has any. My mother doesn't have
to ask about happiness. She already knows who has it.

My grandmother throws out the nurse

No eyelash-batting woman is allowed in my house,
no woman with swaying hips can come through
this door and so whether my grandfather takes his medicine,
whether or not they let someone take out the wash is irrelevant.
And when my grandfather waters the plants
and the neighbor comes to peak at their blooms,
my grandmother proudly declares *There are other fish in the sea,*
articulating each word like flint over the metal gate.
They dress—a suit and a skirt, a ribbon of red lipstick
across my grandmother's lips, my grandfather
with his smooth leather shoes even in winter.
My grandfather, who declares he doesn't fear the cold,
would refuse a winter coat just so he could bask in the sun of style,
on a ride to McDonald's where they unwrapped
the yellow-gold paper around their sandwiches,
let fall a shower of french-fries between cracked seats.
But my grandfather would only take his medicine if the nurse
batted her eyelashes, said his name one too many times.
My mother's the one who told the nurse
He has to be coaxed so my grandmother wasn't
entirely wrong when she put a stop to all that.

My mother spins the compost

One bin is a big black barrel that spins and spins
and one is a barrel for collecting rain water
and there are scattered cups and tubs
amidst the matted grass, half-closed lids
full of tomato rinds and avocado skins.
She shows me what's inside the barrel,
but it's too cold to smell the earth
so I focus my eyes on the back of the bin,
a shifting debris of fruits and vegetables.
Come fall, she's in the yard tossing leaves
and sticks expertly in a bin, gleefully cracking
the frozen skin of the water fountain,
or hauling a glitter of pebbles to make a fairy path.
She used to spend her time hauling rocks,
silver and white, loaded in the car's trunk
then dispersed around the yard.
For a whole year she stopped at every corner
to eye the shape and tone of every stone.
My mother's even laid her own bricks,
now a lopsided path of orange and red,
embedded in the earth's furrowed cheek.
By the slabs of pale and uneven rock,
the thunder of a barrel turning.

Piano Lessons

My mother used to use a pencil
to ensure the fingers' perfect curvature.
Now she believes it's all pure will.
She gives a whack on the back that means
Sit up straight! She takes out my sister's horse whip
to ensure the student is paying attention
before they break out into smiles
and my mother waves the whip again
to say *Wake up!* the tip of the whip frayed
thin into feathers by the bite of the cat.
At the piano my mother's attention is a gift.
I always knew I was prepared when my mother
stopped washing dishes and came into the room.
I braced myself for correction: everything
wrong, even my touch, the way I sit,
the way my shoulders rise like mountains.
Now I'd do anything to avert my mother's attention.
I try to direct her toward someone else's potential,
but on a good day she still folds her hands and waits.

My mother when company comes

Stops speaking to me, or at best speaks
to me in bursts and gusts of unfinished thoughts,
hangs up without saying goodbye,
leaves me guessing as I try to plug in a missing noun or a verb.
Holds the phone like a microphone so others can speak.
She hasn't spoken to me in full sentences in weeks
and when she does it's to tell me to come meet at the mall,
meet at the store. She always tells me to come and I do,
though I start to feel the kaleidoscope-spin of so much rushing.
My mother impatiently twiddles her thumbs in the car,
fiddles with her notebook where she lists appointments
with a script I used to forge at school.
My mother's eyes shift. Out in the yard, my mother
breathes into cupped hands, busies herself with weeds,
collects fallen sticks, huffs a spume of white air.
She eyes the horizon—*a reminder.*
I never could finish my mother's sentences.

On Saturdays we do Alakazoo Schedule

When Cinderella's fairy grandmother gussied her up
for the ball, she sang *Alakazoo kamizi kaboo*
(or something like that) and a million mice came out
of the woodwork to patch, sew, and string.
The birds fluttered a crown together on the princess's
fluffed up head. On Saturdays we played at being mice,
going room to room, cleaning, pressing, and folding.
My father wiped the counters, my mother loaded the wash.
Sometimes I hid in a corner where *Alakazoo*
could not find me, where the train-fast song faded
to the tune of real birds chattering outside my window.
Descending the stairs, I saw entire layers of dirt
and grime being lifted, my mother dropping loads
of laundry onto the ground with a thwack of finality.
We *Alakazoo* today too, giving ourselves time limits
just for the thrill of it, just to see how fast we can go.
We *Alakazoo* out the door and *Alakazoo* home.
I can't live on anything but this even if I'm perpetually behind,
my fairy godmother tisking her wand at me like an angry
orchestra conductor. I chug along *faster faster* though I don't care
if this pumpkin turns into a chariot, these rags into a gauzy gown,
if my glass slippers get smashed into a thousand jagged stars.

My grandmother's cooking

My grandmother cooked the meals when we came to visit.
She made me cream of wheat lumped to perfection,
baked ziti overcooked to perfect softness.
My grandmother cooked for us until she started
substituting chocolate milk for regular,
stirring pieces of vegetables (broccoli, tomato, pepper),
a rainbow of colors swirled into the mashed potatoes,
though I was happy to turn my pasta into dessert,
to find streaks of color in unlikely places.
Later, my grandmother would sit and be served at our table.
I remember she had the poise of a queen.
A tranquil smile on her face. A red scarf around her neck.
Until she'd bang her fist on the table and say
(stretching the last word into multiple syllables) *It's time to eat!*

Fear of Falling

I walk the frozen path of crushed ice dampening the sidewalk,
islands of cold I crush into water beneath my feet.
Coldness I want to smash to oblivion the way
my mother marches up and down over the gutter
where snow is caked above the grates.
My mother marches up and down in stiff jolts,
slides chunks of ice into the black vent as cars go by,
heads turning to wonder and wave.
It's her version of public safety—
to stop everything stagnant, everything that waits.
She turns away from a sure-footed woman,
white-haired and ambling over ice.
My mother can't bear the thought of a body falling,
though the only thing she truly fears
is the slow ricochet of my grandfather's last fall.
No way to know how all those cuts, bruises,
and scrapes scattered everywhere, a swirl of damage
from a single fall in a slick parking lot.
My mother averts her eyes no matter how sure
a body slinking over ice, no matter how carefully
each leg lifts, arms outstretched for perfect balance,
so every day I break the ice to bits.

My mother always has something for me

A box. A jar of tomato sauce.
And if she has nothing she finds out
what I need or thinks of something I ought to have.
On Saturday mornings, I used to fly down
the stairs, and we would race to yard sales.
We still go to yard sales and thrift stores too,
where my mother finds me a suitcase
still tagged with someone else's address,
a crumpled red ribbon that still shines.
I imagine the suitcase tumbling onto
the conveyor belt, the feeling of home
as it cruises toward familiar hands.
A flurry of comings and goings.
All the things my mother gives me
makes me feel like I'm going somewhere,
like I'm getting ready for something too.
I cradle the jar of tomato sauce,
the regifted box of chocolate truffles,
four oranges in a paper bag.
I roll the suitcase toward its new home.
Tell it things won't be so different here.

My mother cuts fruit and vegetables daily

slices of onion and tomatoes all cut with the same knife,
yellow slabs of pineapple so sweet they look translucent
with the slickness of pure sugar. She tosses chunks
 of lettuce in a bowl, salad dressing smeared on the counter.
Adds more and more sliced tomatoes.
My mother says *Tomatoes are good for your face.*
She also says *Rain is good for your skin*
so I tilt my face to the sky,
pop extra tomatoes onto my plate.
There is something for everything that ails you
but I've never loved to quantify,
never been one to think through each problem
and I don't care about anything other than taste.
My mother is unphased by the stickiness
running down her arms, unphased by work.
Now, in the kitchen she cracks open a pomegranate
undaunted by the red beads clinging to rind,
rubies she showers into a bowl and hands to me.

My mother means business

She believes in a hundred and one pursuits,
a new enterprise for each day.
She finds busted boxes in store aisles
 at night and collects them for me
so I can ship a top, a dress, some pants
 to California, Texas, Alabama.
My mother has waited years to sell my prom dresses,
1950s artifacts with crinoline slips and gauzy sleeves,
layers of silver tulle, two thick roses
curled like fists on the skirt.
I want to unfurl them, lay those stiff petals flat.
My mother helped me find this dress
in a small boutique, the day hugging us close
with grayness and heavy clouds.
So many emotions inside of me.
I wish I could ship *those* somewhere too,
package and postmark everything inside me.
We scoop it in a bag, lay flat the voluminous gauze,
fold the box like we're closing a window—
the dress I'm shipping to Arkansas.

On my father's birthday my mother cuts meat from the bone

She can't stop asking which dish he likes best
and because we are all sharing the meal,
he has bites from each plate to help him decide.
My mother slices the meat from the shank
and I cut pieces of charred lamb, juices
oozing into the pile of rice and my mother suddenly
lifts the entire bone to her plate. I don't know
if or how long she holds the bone to her lips
to eat the remaining slivers because I've seen my mother
pick at so many bones. I also like to nibble
at the edge of things, to feel the need and abundance,
wanting to take it all in but leave everything out.
I don't know synchronicity but if a choir
(so I'm told) synchronizes its heartbeats in song,
then a good meal brings us closer to the true pulse of things.
At the end, my mother asks if we can keep the sauce
from my father's plate. I catch each drop and scoop
the leftover bread into a bag, though each bite
won't feel the same tomorrow in the quiet of the kitchen.
Before we go, we finish squares of baklava on the house,
mounds of whipped cream powdered with pistachios.
Everything disappears so fast.

Such a Baby

I ask my mother for her first impression of my father.
She says *He was such a baby,*
but my mother is a baby too.
She hates spicy food, shakes her head
as she swigs a glass of milk
to cool the heat prickling her lips.
She's been known to eat the gooey
center of a pie and leave the crust.
At the salon, my mother leaves
before even two hairs are plucked.
When she gets her hair done,
she brings a million things to do.
Sitting with her phone and agenda book,
she's like a horse banging at the stall to be let out.
In my parents' wedding photo, my father
is wearing a fitted, powder blue suit.
My mother's curls are soft and fluffy.
Her sleeves tumble past her shoulders,
fixed in a forever slow-fall,
her shoulders and collarbones thin as bird's wings.
Though I can't remember seeing a picture
of my mother as an actual baby
and though I can't see her eyes as she closes them
to embrace my father, this feels like the closest thing.

My mother on vacation

calls me more than you'd expect.
She makes a concession.
Decides to sit on a bench to watch the waves roll in.
Knowing her, she does this for my father
who loves, more than anything,
the wake of breaking waves,
the curve of the coast tapering towards the horizon.
At dinner in the dim-lit restaurant,
my mother carves the meat from the bone
without realizing she's kept nothing but fat.
That night when she starts feeling sick,
I tell my mother to *Pay attention!*
I say it over and over until I feel guilty.
I keep saying *Pay attention, pay attention*
though if she did, she wouldn't be my mother.

My Mother's Song

When my mother hugs me, she thumps me
two three times on the back. Hard.
My mother yells *Drop your shoulders!*
to my father when he plays the piano.
With each line, his shoulders rise with tension.
She's probably thumped his shoulders too.
When my mother is at the piano, she has no worries except
finding the next note, the next page of music.
She plays samples for the piano students,
asks them which ones they like best.
Growing up, I always heard her play the same song.
A song that sometimes sounded like a chandelier
crashing to the ground. Sometimes like a sumptuous party
softening into closed doors and velvet curtains at midnight.
Then the party would be over and she would
jump from the bench to tell us to practice.
Today I hear her students play the same song
with the same force, a sudden crash and shimmer.
The descending thump of jagged chords.
A song I didn't think anyone could play but her.

I don't know if my mother always loved horses

or if she just loves them because my sister does.
My mother made us ride because we were shy.
If you can tame a horse you can tame anything.
But we still whispered into our teacher's ears.
Were too scared to ask to use the bathroom.
When I got a blue ribbon riding my pony,
she let me quit but my sister continued.
My sister says she loves the dust, the smell of hay,
even mucking out a dirty stall.
When we used to play pretend, she was always
 sixteen with a black mare she tamed herself.
Today my mother rushes to the barn to watch my sister
canter around the ring, hooves kicking up towers of dust.
My father stands outside trying to clear his allergies.
And that's where I stand too. Trying to wipe my eyes and nose,
breathing the fresh air of the blurry, tear-stained hills.
I only came to see if a fox might cross our path,
to see what the barnyard cats were up to.
My mother is still the one who tells everyone what to do
though I'm not sure she ever got a horse to listen.

Comfortable Night

Two heads with twisted curls crowded into bed
the way my sister and I used to.
My aunt declared it *Comfortable Night*
and that meant she and my mother shared a bed.
My aunt would gleefully stretch onto my mother's side
and squeeze her in a hug all night,
her chin pressed into my mother's shoulder.
I've never known my mother to shrink from touch
but I know she hates to feel trapped just as much as I do.
Comfortable Night went on and on for many years,
and as the youngest sister she let her big sister
share the bed until one day she wised up enough to say *Enough.*
My sister too shared my room because she hated to be alone.
She used to follow me around the house playing
her untuned violin, begging me to play a duet
of screeching scales which was all that we could muster.
My mother still hates to feel trapped.
At the lake, she looks out the fogged window
with her fingers curled behind her back.
I can tell she's anxious, feeling trapped,
though it's Sunday and there isn't anything to do.
I know my mother is only comfortable
when she has her own space, a piano student at the door,
a fully booked day, and a world of space to do it in.

My mother at the exhibition

The room swirls with garlands and banners,
paintings of kites and flowers on the walls
 and to the side my painting of pears,
unnamed, unsigned, the way I like it.
I'm thankful my painting has a corner
to lean on, the place I'd most like to stand.
My mother helps herself to two brownies,
three slices of tomato with cheese,
refills her cup several times,
leans the glass water dispenser on its side
until every drop leaks and the empty crystal shines.
My mother does one, two, three rounds
of the open room and side gallery,
pointing too closely at everything.
I ignore her jabs at first, testing my ability to resist
until she hisses, fills out my name tag herself.
My mother doesn't want anyone given short shrift,
as if after all these years of my sister asking
Why didn't you ever brag about us?,
my mother could make up for it now.
In pictures anyone can recognize my mother's writing,
the uneven letters scrawled across my chest
and I'm glad not to see my own print, letters bubbly
as balloon animals I wish could float away.

My mother tells me to write

Because of all the creative ways I've wished for it to end,
because of all the flowery ways I've complained,
because something comes of nothing and nothing comes
of something and productivity means pulling opportunity
out of thin air. My mother believes in advancement.
My grandfather used to say *If you are stupid you won't live long.*
Would declare himself rich if he had money
in his pocket and gas in his car. Distance was a dare.
My grandfather drove my grandmother from Florida
to New York so many times I forgot what they looked like
until they gave me a picture to go with the sea-shell figurine
reclining on a plastic hammock from a beachside gift shop.
When they gave me the photo, it was the first time I realized
memory could fail. My mother tells me to write because
Nothing good comes of all that thinking round and round
(the way she's twiddling her thumbs now) or roving up and down
like my grandfather firing up the engine and leaving town.

Esther Sadoff is a teacher and writer from Columbus, Ohio. Her poems have been featured or are forthcoming in *Up the Staircase Quarterly, Hole in the Head Review, Little Patuxent Review, Jet Fuel Review, Cathexis Poetry Northwest, Pidgeonholes, Red Ogre Review, South Florida Poetry Journal,* among others. She is the author of several forthcoming chapbooks: *Serendipity in France,* Finishing Line Press; *Dear Silence,* Kelsay Books, and *If I Hold My Breath,* Bottlecap Press. She was nominated for a Pushcart in 2023 by *Hole in the Head Review.*